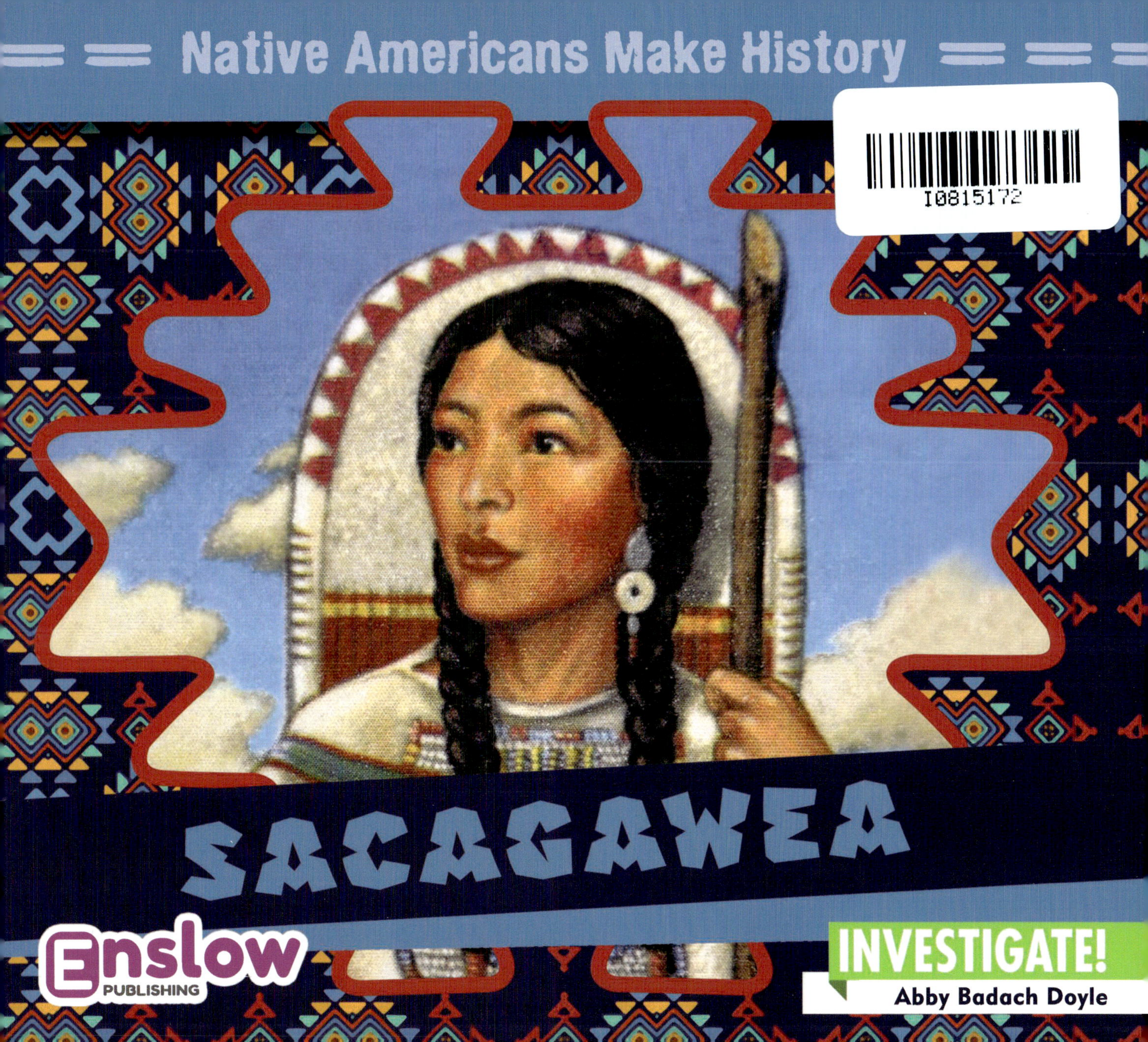
Native Americans Make History
I0815172
SACAGAWEA
Enslow PUBLISHING
INVESTIGATE!
Abby Badach Doyle

Please visit our website, www.enslow.com. For a free color catalog of all our high-quality books, call toll free 1-800-398-2504 or fax 1-877-980-4454.

Library of Congress Cataloging-in-Publication Data
Names: Doyle, Abby Badach, author.
Title: Sacagawea / Abby Badach Doyle.
Description: New York : Enslow Publishing, [2023] | Series: Native Americans make history | Includes bibliographical references and index.
Identifiers: LCCN 2021054208 (print) | LCCN 2021054209 (ebook) | ISBN 9781978527768 (library binding) | ISBN 9781978527744 (paperback) | ISBN 9781978527751 (set) | ISBN 9781978527775 (ebook)
Subjects: LCSH: Sacagawea–Juvenile literature. | Lewis and Clark Expedition (1804-1806)–Biography–Juvenile literature. | Shoshoni Indians–Biography–Juvenile literature. | Shoshoni women–Biography–Juvenile literature.
Classification: LCC F592.7.S12 D69 2023 (print) | LCC F592.7.S12 (ebook) | DDC 978.004/9745740092 [B]–dc23/eng/20211123
LC record available at https://lccn.loc.gov/2021054208
LC ebook record available at https://lccn.loc.gov/2021054209

Portions of this work were originally authored by Caitie McAneney and published as *The Life of Sacagawea*. All new material in this edition is authored by Abby Badach Doyle.

Published in 2023 by
Enslow Publishing
29 E. 21st Street
New York, NY 10010

Designer: Leslie Taylor
Editor: Abby Badach Doyle

Photo credits: cover, p. 7, 29 neftali/Shutterstock.com; (series artwork) Nevada31/Shutterstock.com; (series font/artwork) Alhovik/Shutterstock.com; p. 5 https://commons.wikimedia.org/wiki/File:Detail_Lewis_%26_Clark_at_Three_Forks.jpg; p. 7 https://commons.wikimedia.org/wiki/File:Shoshoni_tipis.jpg; p. 9 (Charbonneau) https://en.wikipedia.org/wiki/File:Charbonneau_Painting_Cropped.jpg; p. 9 (village) https://commons.wikimedia.org/wiki/File:Winter_village_of_the_Minatarres_0059v.jpg; p. 11 (map) https://commons.wikimedia.org/wiki/File:Lewis_and_Clark_Expedition_map.svg; p. 13 https://commons.wikimedia.org/wiki/File:International university lectures, delivered by the most distinguished representatives of the greatest universities of the world, at the Congress of arts and science, Universal exposition, St. Louis . (14789271243).jpg; p. 15 (river), 25 (photo) Teresa Otto/Shutterstock.com; p. 15 (statue) K_Z/Shutterstock.com; p. 17 (Beaverhead Rock) https://commons.wikimedia.org/wiki/File:%22The_overland_stage_road_between_Ogden_and_Helena_crossing_the_Beaver_Head_River_at_Point_of_Rocks_..._by_means_of_a_pla_-_NARA_-_520085.tif; p. 17 (map) Schwabenblitz/Shutterstock.com; p. 19 (painting) https://commons.wikimedia.org/wiki/File:Lewis_and_Clark_Reach_Shoshone_Camp_Led_by_Sacajawea.jpg; p. 19 (Lewis) Evertt Collection/Shutterstock.com; p. 21 (canoe) https://commons.wikimedia.org/wiki/File:Dugout_Canoe_(Clatsop_County,_Oregon_scenic_images)_(clatDA0092).jpg; p. 21 (painting) https://commons.wikimedia.org/wiki/File:Lewis_and_clark-expedition.jpg; p. 23 https://commons.wikimedia.org/wiki/File:Fort_Clatsop,_OR_(Lewis_and_Clarks%27_Winter_Camp)_9-1-13la_(10004011004).jpg; p. 25 https://commons.wikimedia.org/wiki/File:Popi_sig550.jpg; p. 27 Dimitrios Karamitros/Shutterstock.com; p. 29 (coins) Daniel D Malone/Shutterstock; p. 29 (statue) Joseph Sohm/Shutterstock.com.

Printed in the United States of America

CPSIA compliance information: Batch #CSENS23: For further information contact Enslow Publishing, New York, New York, at 1-800-398-2504.

CONTENTS

Words in the glossary appear in **bold** type the first time they are used in the text.

STRONG LIKE A GIRL

In 1804, Meriwether Lewis and William Clark began a famous trip to **explore** the American West. On foot and by boat, they journeyed around 15 to 20 miles (24 to 32 km) per day. They traveled over tall mountains and roaring rivers. Some days there was barely any food to eat.

Now imagine doing all that . . . but as the only teenage girl in a group of adult men. And you're carrying your newborn baby on your back! That's what Sacagawea did. More than 200 years later, we still remember her bravery and strength.

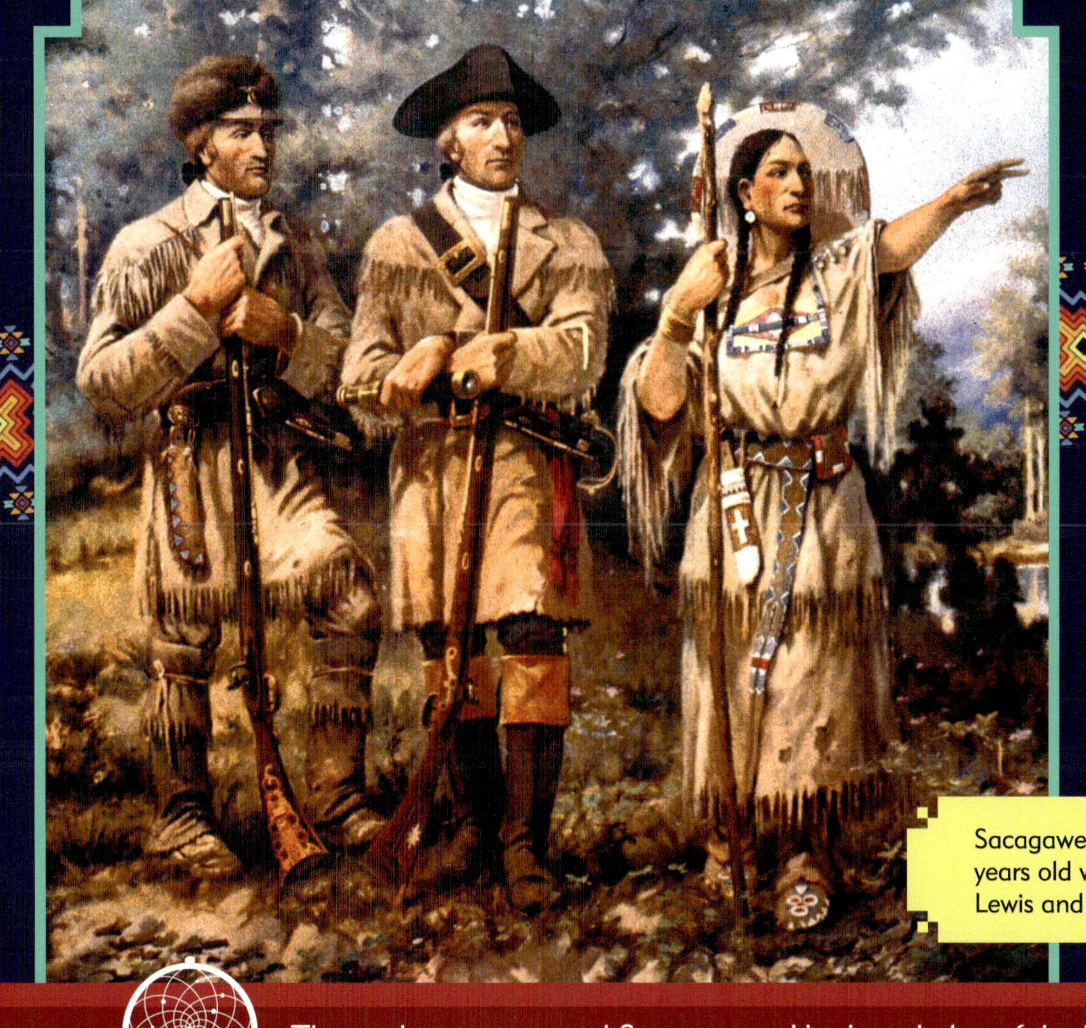

Sacagawea was 16 or 17 years old when she joined Lewis and Clark.

Explore More!

The explorers respected Sacagawea. Her knowledge of the land was necessary on their long journey. She knew what plants could be eaten for food or to heal sickness. She also spoke the language of the Shoshone and Hidatsa groups they met along the way.

EARLY LIFE

Sacagawea means "bird woman" in Hidatsa. It's also spelled Sacajawea which means "boat launcher" in the Shoshone language. Launch means to push. Little is known about her early life. Historians, or people who study history, think she may have been born around 1788.

Sacagawea was born into the Lemhi Shoshone Tribe. When Sacagawea was alive, there were four major groups of Shoshone people. They lived across what is now the western United States, in present-day California, Nevada, Utah, Idaho, and Wyoming. Sacagawea grew up in what is now Idaho near its border with Montana.

Sacagawea's people, the Lemhi Shoshone, were a band of the Northern Shoshone. They lived in tepees.

Explore More!

During Sacagawea's time, each of the four Shoshone groups spoke different **dialects** of the same language. That means that even with small differences in the way they spoke, members of different Shoshone groups could still understand each other.

KIDNAPPED!

In 1800, an enemy tribe, the Hidatsa, captured Sacagawea during a raid, or surprise attack. The Hidatsa war party forced Sacagawea out of her home and took her to their village in modern-day North Dakota. She was only about 12 years old.

As a young teenager, Sacagawea was sold as a slave to a French-Canadian fur trader named Toussaint Charbonneau (too-SAHNT SHAR-boh-noh). Even though Charbonneau was much older, he made Sacagawea his wife. He was also married to another Shoshone woman who had been captured. They lived together in a Hidatsa village called Metaharta.

Toussaint Charbonneau

This artwork shows what a Hidatsa village looked like in Sacagawea's time.

Explore More!

Life with the Hidatsa was different from life with the Shoshone. The Shoshone followed the bison and lived in tepees, which were easy to move. The Hidatsa grew crops and made fixed villages. They lived in dome-shaped homes made of soil.

THE ADVENTURE BEGINS

Meanwhile, a major event happened in the young United States. In 1803, the new country doubled in size when it gained 828,000 square miles (2,144,510 sq km) of land from the French. This was known as the Louisiana Purchase. At the time, this was more land than anyone could imagine!

President Thomas Jefferson put together an **expedition** to explore the newly bought land. He wanted to map its features and borders, as well as learn about the people, animals, and plants living there. He hired Meriwether Lewis to lead the expedition. Lewis asked William Clark to be his partner.

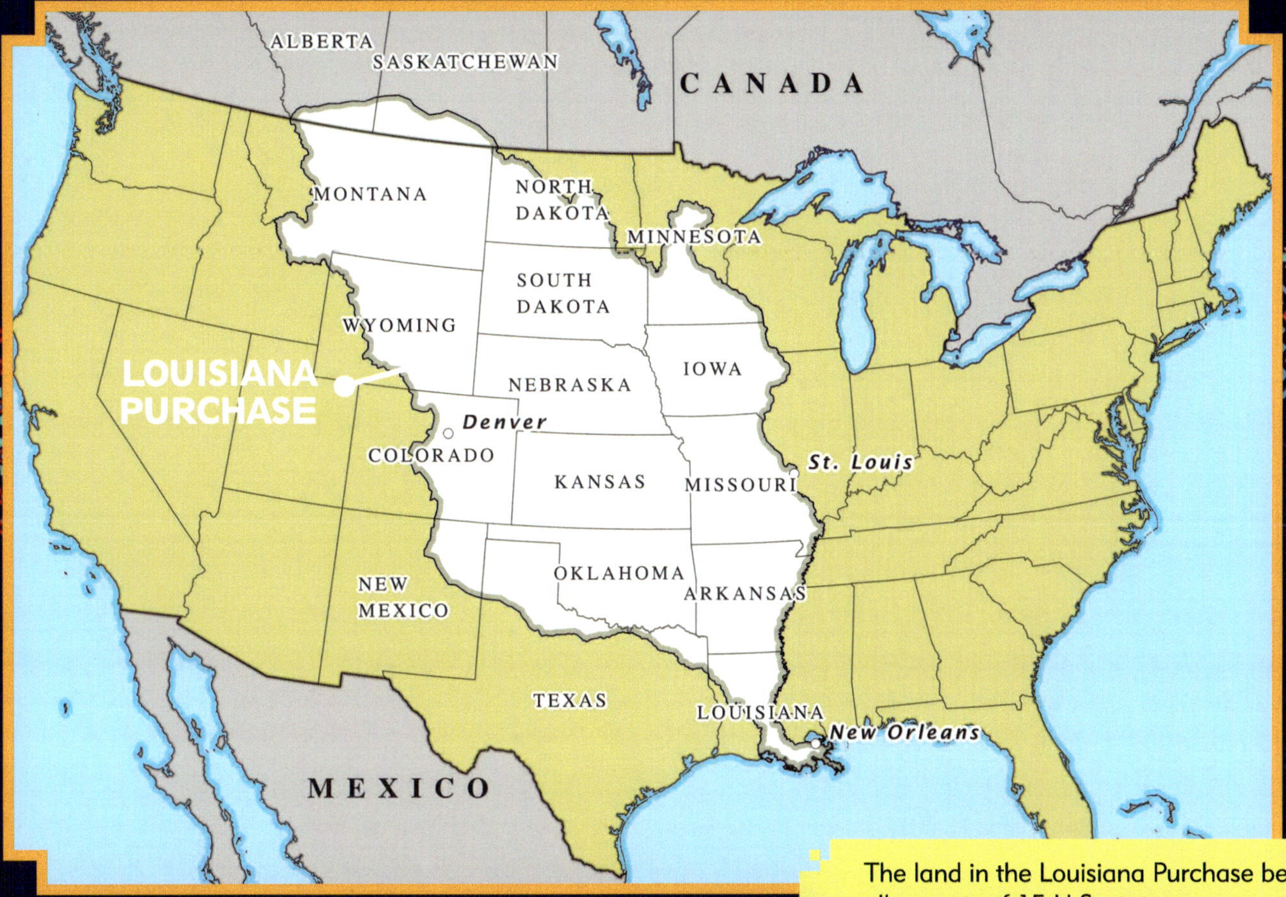

ALBERTA
SASKATCHEWAN
CANADA
MONTANA
NORTH DAKOTA
MINNESOTA
SOUTH DAKOTA
WYOMING
LOUISIANA PURCHASE
IOWA
NEBRASKA
Denver
COLORADO
St. Louis
KANSAS
MISSOURI
NEW MEXICO
OKLAHOMA
ARKANSAS
TEXAS
LOUISIANA
New Orleans
MEXICO

The land in the Louisiana Purchase became all or parts of 15 U.S. states.

Lewis and Clark, both U.S. Army veterans, led a team of 40 to 50 men. They called their team the Corps of Discovery. Corps, spoken as "KOR," is a military term for an orderly group of people doing something together.

MEETING LEWIS AND CLARK

In December 1803, the Corps of Discovery made a camp near where the Mississippi and Missouri Rivers meet. Here, they prepared for their journey. That spring, they left St. Louis, Missouri, and traveled west. By a stroke of luck, they met Sacagawea at a Hidatsa village in what is now North Dakota.

Sacagawea's husband Charbonneau spoke Hidatsa and French. He suggested he and Sacagawea join the Corps of Discovery to help **translate**. This was important to the crew, who needed to speak Sacagawea's Shoshone language to buy horses for their journey.

Sacagawea's presence as a woman showed that the Corps of Discovery came in peace.

Explore More!

Sacagawea didn't speak English but could translate the Shoshone language into Hidatsa. Her husband could translate Hidatsa into French. A member of the Corps of Discovery, François Labiche, spoke French and English. He translated the French to English for the other crew members.

SACAGAWEA SAVES THE DAY

Only one month into their trip, one of the Corps of Discovery's boats nearly sank. It hit a burst of wind while Charbonneau was steering. The boat carried important papers, instruments, supplies, and **medicine**. It also held all the journals Lewis and Clark wrote with their observations of the land.

Sacagawea helped right away. While others panicked, she stayed calm and gathered the valued items before they got washed away in the river. Sacagawea even dove into the water! To thank her, Lewis and Clark named a **tributary** of the Musselshell River after her.

Musselshell River

Sacagawea was known to carry her baby on her back.

Explore More!

Sacagawea gave birth to a son in February 1805, just about two months before joining the Corps of Discovery on their journey. She named her baby Jean Baptiste and he joined them for the expedition. Clark nicknamed him "Pomp" or "Pompey."

BACK IN HER HOMELAND

It was now August 1805. The Lewis and Clark expedition reached the Continental Divide, a mountain ridge in western North America. The Corps of Discovery needed to meet the Shoshone to buy horses soon. The next leg of their journey would take them through the steep Rocky Mountains, and they needed horses to help carry supplies.

The land was starting to look familiar to Sacagawea. It was the land of her childhood. She recognized Beaverhead Rock, in what is now Montana. She knew the Shoshone must be near.

MONTANA

Beaverhead Rock

The Shoshone named Beaverhead Rock for its **resemblance** to the animal.

Divide means to break up. The Continental Divide separates the flow of water to the Atlantic and Pacific Oceans. To the west, all water drains into the Pacific Ocean. To the east, water ends up in the Gulf of Mexico and the Atlantic Ocean.

MEETING THE SHOSHONE

On August 12, Lewis and a small group crossed the Continental Divide at Lemhi Pass. They met the Shoshone and, as a sign of peace, removed their shoes. They then smoked a peace pipe. Five days later, Sacagawea and the rest of the expedition joined them.

She then came face to face with the band of Shoshone she had been born into. To Sacagawea's surprise, their chief was now her brother Cameahwait! It was a joyful reunion for everyone. As planned, Sacagawea spoke the Shoshone language and helped the expedition get horses for their journey.

Lewis in Shoshone clothing

Chief Cameahwait gave Lewis a tippet, which is a wrap made of otter skin.

Explore More!

The Shoshone were **suspicious** of Lewis at first. Few, if any, white settlers had ever traveled to their land. At the time, raids were common between unfriendly groups. When Sacagawea arrived, with her baby on her back, it was clear they came in peace.

ACROSS THE MOUNTAINS

In late August 1805, the Corps of Discovery left the Shoshone to continue their journey into the steep and **dangerous** Bitterroot Mountains. About a month later, the expedition reached the other side in present-day Idaho. Tired and hungry, they found a village of the Nez Percé. This friendly tribe taught them how to make canoes out of trees.

They used these canoes to travel down the Clearwater and Snake Rivers. By mid-October, they had reached the Columbia River. This was a huge landmark because it is a major waterway leading to the Pacific Ocean.

In present-day Washington State, the Columbia and Snake Rivers meet at Sacajawea Historical State Park.

dugout tree canoe

Explore More!

Sacagawea's name is spelled about 15 different ways in the journals of Lewis and Clark. Mostly, they used the Hidatsa spelling "Sacagawea" instead of the Shoshone spelling "Sacajawea," which has the additional meaning "she who carries a burden," or load.

REACHING THE PACIFIC

The Lewis and Clark expedition reached the Pacific Ocean in November 1805. However, winter was upon them. They needed to build a camp to wait until around springtime to journey back east. The expedition took a vote on where to build winter lodging.

Sacagawea was allowed to share her opinion too. Once a Hidatsa war prisoner and slave, this young woman now had a voice the men of the expedition considered. They built Fort Clatsop, named for the Clatsop Tribe who lived nearby. Today it's near Astoria, Oregon.

A replica, or close copy, of Fort Clatsop stands at the site today.

Explore More!

In January 1806, members of the Clatsop Tribe visited the camp. They said a big whale washed up on the beach! Clark wanted to find it. Sacagawea **insisted** she go too. Only bones remained when they arrived, but she got to see the Pacific Ocean.

ENDING THE ADVENTURE

That winter, the explorers wrote and drew maps in their journals. They also boiled ocean water and saved the leftover salt. The salt helped keep meat from going bad. Finally, the Corps of Discovery packed up and headed home in March 1806.

As they passed through Shoshone lands, Sacagawea remembered a trail from her childhood, now called Bozeman Pass. It runs through the southwestern part of present-day Montana. She said this was an easier route than the way Clark wanted to go, and she was right! In his journal, he called her his "pilot" which means guide.

Clark cut his name into the rock near Pompeys Pillar, pictured here.

Explore More!

On their journey home, Clark noticed a large rock formation. He named it Pompy's Tower, after the nickname he gave to Sacagawea's son Jean Baptiste. Now known as Pompeys Pillar, you can visit this landmark today in Yellowstone County, Montana.

In August 1806, the expedition returned to the Hidatsa village where they first met Sacagawea. Her journey was now over. Sacagawea's husband Charbonneau received around $500 to $800 and more than 300 acres (121 ha) of land for his help. Sacagawea herself did not receive any payment.

Less is written about Sacagawea's life after the expedition. In 1809, she and Charbonneau moved to Missouri to become farmers. It didn't work out, so in 1811, they moved out west again when Charbonneau took a translator job with the Missouri Fur Company.

The Lewis and Clark Expedition

North Dakota
Mississippi River
Fort Clatsop
Route of Lewis and Clark Expedition
Washington D.C.
ATLANTIC OCEAN
Missouri
PACIFIC OCEAN

Lewis and Clark's expedition covered more than 8,000 miles (12,875 km).

Explore More!

Sacagawea and Charbonneau remained good friends with William Clark. In 1809, they traveled to St. Louis, Missouri, to **baptize** their son Jean Baptiste. There, they left him in Clark's care when they decided to return west. Clark also paid for Jean Baptiste's education.

REMEMBERING SACAGAWEA

In August 1812, Sacagawea had a daughter named Lisette. That December, it was reported that Charbonneau's wife died in South Dakota. Since Charbonneau had more than one wife, this could have been another woman. However, most historians believe it was Sacagawea. She was only 24 or 25 years old.

There is a lot we will never know about Sacagawea. Fortunately, we have many written stories about her on the Lewis and Clark expedition. Her gentle nature and knowledge of the land helped them greatly. Some even say the expedition would have failed without her.

One Shoshone account says Sacagawea returned to her Shoshone people and lived to almost 100!

Sacagawea golden dollar coin

THE LIFE OF SACAGAWEA

circa (around) 1788	circa 1800	1804	February 11, 1805	August 17, 1805	March 1806	August 1806	August 1812	December 1812	1884
Sacagawea is born to the Lemhi Shoshone Tribe in present-day Idaho.	Sacagawea is kidnapped by the Hidatsa Tribe and enslaved.	Toussaint Charbonneau buys Sacagawea and makes her his wife. In November, Sacagawea meets the Lewis and Clark expedition.	Sacagawea gives birth to her first child, Jean Baptiste. Two months later, they set off on the Corps of Discovery expedition.	Sacagawea reunites with her brother, Chief Cameahwait.	Sacagawea and the expedition begin their journey home.	Sacagawea's journey ends when she returns to the Mandan-Hidatsa village in present-day North Dakota.	Sacagawea gives birth to her second child, Lisette.	One of Charbonneau's wives dies of a fever. She may have been Sacagawea.	A Shoshone woman dies on the Wind River **Reservation**. Some believe she was the real Sacagawea.

Explore More!

A picture of Sacagawea was never made while she was alive. Even so, her likeness is found on coins, artwork, statues, and even stamps. In 2001, President Bill Clinton honored Sacagawea by naming her an honorary sergeant, or officer, in the U.S. Army.

GLOSSARY

baptize: To have a special service to make someone a member of a church.

dangerous: Unsafe.

dialect: A form of a language that is local to a certain area, with its own words and manner of speaking.

expedition: A trip made for a certain purpose.

explore: To search in order to find out new things.

insist: To ask for something in a strong way.

medicine: A drug taken to make a sick person well.

resemblance: The state of looking like something else.

reservation: A piece of land set aside by the U.S. government for Native Americans to live.

suspicious: Having a feeling that someone is behaving wrongly.

translate: To change words and phrases from one language into another language.

tributary: A river that joins a larger river or a lake.

FOR MORE INFORMATION

Books

Buckley Jr., James. *Sacagawea: Courageous Trailblazer!* San Diego, CA: Portable Press, 2021.

Byers, Ann. *Sacagawea.* New York, NY: Cavendish Square, 2020.

Olson, Gillia M. *The Life of Sacagawea.* Mankato, MN: Amicus Ink, 2021.

Websites

Sacagawea
ducksters.com/biography/explorers/sacagawea.php
Read interesting facts about Sacagawea and how she helped the Lewis and Clark expedition.

Sacagawea
kids.britannica.com/kids/article/Sacagawea/353736
See photos of stamps and coins with Sacagawea on them and learn more about her life.

Woman Heroes: Sacagawea
kids.nationalgeographic.com/history/article/sacagawea
See famous paintings of Sacagawea and read about her life.

INDEX